Build Fun AI Projects that Run on
Volume 1: PyScript, GitHub, and ... ...

Build Fun AI Projects that Run on the Web

Volume 1: PyScript, GitHub, and KNN

Ricardo A. Calix

Dedication

To my family

Contents

Dedication   v

Preface   xi

1 Introduction   **1**
1.1   Complete list of Tools and Technologies   2
1.2   GitHub   3
     1.2.1   Creating Account with GitHub   3
     1.2.2   Creating and Editing Folders and Files on GitHub   4
     1.2.3   Configuring GitHub Pages   10
1.3   HTML   14
1.4   JavaScript   14
1.5   PyScript   15
1.6   Python   16
1.7   Numpy   17
1.8   Pandas   18
1.9   Data   19
1.10   What is KNN anyway?   20
1.11   Resources   23
1.12   Conclusion   23

2 Coding with HTML and PyScript   **25**
2.1   Hello World program with HTML and PyScript   25
2.2   The Power of Numpy and PyScript   31
2.3   Solve these Problems   48
     2.3.1   Problem 1   49
     2.3.2   Problem 2   49
     2.3.3   Problem 3   50
     2.3.4   Problem 4   50
     2.3.5   Problem 5   51
     2.3.6   Problem 6   51
     2.3.7   Problem 7   52
     2.3.8   Problem 8   53
2.4   Conclusion   54

3 Build your AI Project with KNN and PyScript   **55**

    3.1   Basics to get KNN running   57

    3.2   A KNN app for Iris Flower classification   71

    3.3   Conclusion   75

4 Final Conclusions   **77**

    4.1   Where to go from here?   78

Other Books by Ricardo A. Calix   **79**

The Author: Ricardo A. Calix   **81**

Glossary   **83**

Bibliography   **85**

An Important Final Note   **87**

Preface

 The early bird catches the worm.

I love to tinker in my basement. I am always building puzzles, clocks, electronics kits, RC planes, recently I 3D printed an Antikythera, etc. You get the picture. I just like to learn by doing and building. In my professional life I practice data science consulting and teach about AI and machine learning at a University. For years I have looked for fun AI projects one can build and learn from similar to my previously described basement hobbies. However, I have not found many. This is probably because of the nature of AI and machine learning. In the past, you needed lots of tools to install on your computer, didn't really know where to even begin, and you basically reported lots of statistics about the trained AI models. But you didn't have that rewarding feeling of building something like with RC planes or hobby electronics. This, however, is about to change thanks to PyScript and other tools being made available everyday.

With PyScript you can now build and learn about AI and machine learning, and you can also do it all in the web browser with just GitHub. And the fun aspect of this is that when you are done with your project, you will have a working AI tool that runs in the web from anywhere. Wow! What a time we live in. So, since I could not find these AI hobby projects as I wanted them, I decided to build them. This book is the first one in a series of AI project books I plan to create. Hopefully, now your list and my list of home hobby projects will also include AI models that run on the Web!

Ricardo A. Calix, Ph.D.

Greater Chicago Area, USA, August 2, 2023

1 Introduction

This is the first in a series of AI project books that I plan to write. While in the future I want the books to be self contained, this book is definitely the most basic. It is meant to teach all the topics needed for someone who does not know much about AI and/or software. If you are more advanced in your knowledge, I recommend that you skim through the first chapter and then read through the more PyScript focused sections in chapters 2 and 3.

Objective: To be able to build an AI tool that runs on the web.

The goal of this project work book is to help the reader to be able to build and run an AI project that runs on the web. I will do my best to explain all the parts involved and emphasize what are the machine learning parts vs. the web development, infrastructure, or support parts. Basically, what we are trying to do is to deploy a machine learning algorithm that does something on a web browser. To be able to do this, we need an AI algorithm which takes inputs and produces outputs. We also need the infrastructure that allows us to interact with the AI algorithm which in this case is HTML and PyScript.

Finally, we need the environment where everything runs. Here, any browser such as Safari, Edge, Firefox, etc. should do it. And we need a way to edit and host the files. For that, we will use GitHub. Of course, you need a computer with internet access and a browser. Any computer and any internet should do it.

I have included an image of the book cover in the next figure. To me, the book cover encapsulates exactly my intention for each of the volumes in this series. Each volume focuses on one AI methodology, one project, and all the background I think you need to complete it. I hope each work book is fun and that at the end you have a completed project that you can share with your friends and family. This book project can be completed by a person or family in one or 2 weekends. You do not need to purchase any kits, and your laptop should be all you need. Any supplementary materials should be available from the official course repo or my website.

Figure 1.1: Cover

1.1 Complete list of Tools and Technologies

To build and run the AI project in this work book you will need to use several technological tools. Most of what you need is software. For the project you will be working with code and writing software. However, coding means using several different modules that all work together to achieve a specific goal. Most of the book will focus on introducing these software modules. First, I will explain and provide examples of the different modules. It will be important to understand what they are for and how to use them independently. Then, we will need to combine them to build and run our project. GitHub, which I will describe shortly is a platform for hosting code. Like an Instagram but instead of sharing pictures you can share code, blog posts, web pages, etc. GitHub will be very important to deploy our projects.

Some of the tools and technologies that we will need or can use include:

- GitHub
- HTML
- JavaScript
- PyScript
- Numpy
- Python
- Pandas
- Fisher's Iris Dataset

KNN which is our AI/machine learning algorithm, will be built and deployed using these previously listed tools. In the next subsections, I will provide brief descriptions of each of these software tools and technologies.

1.2 GitHub

GitHub is an amazing on line platform. It allows you to upload code, and create files describing your code. These files can be formatted and you can create very impressive pages describing your code. All of that is available through the web of course. GitHub also allows you to create your own websites using the url they create for you or even using your own domain name. This feature is called Pages. GitHub is how you will host, and publish your AI tool on the web. You could also do this by installing web hosting software on your computer or using your own cloud service, but GitHub is cooler.

To use GitHub to Run your AI project on the web you will need to set up an account with them, create some files with some code, and configure Pages to view your finished AI tool. I will describe these 3 task in the next sections. So, yes, we can basically do everything in the GitHub site without having to install anything else.

1.2.1 Creating Account with GitHub

First we need to create our GitHub account. We can do this by visiting the GitHub website. Once there, click on sign up. You should get a screen that looks like the one on the following figure. In the sign up sheet, you will follow the steps that are common when you sign up to any on-line service such as providing your name, email, and setting up a password.

Figure 1.2: GitHub Sign Up

In the next section we will learn how to create files and folders on GitHub.

1.2.2 Creating and Editing Folders and Files on GitHub

Once you have created your account and completed the sign up on GitHub, you can proceed to create your repository (usually called a repo) on GitHub. The steps should be as follows. Go to the top menu on the main page and click on repositories. Then you can click on the green button that says new on the upper right hand corner as can be seen in the figure below.

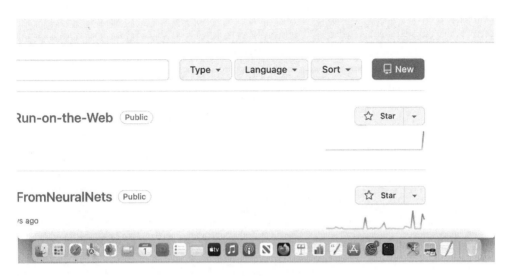

Figure 1.3: Create New Repo

Now in the text box after your user name, you can add the name for your new repo. As can be seen in the next figure, you can type any name you want. Do not use spaces and instead consider using dashes.

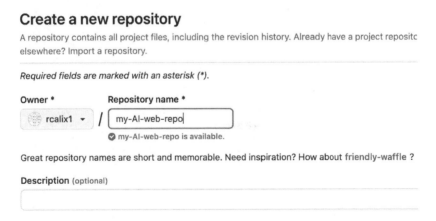

Figure 1.4: My AI Web Repo

GitHub will check that the name is available. Once it is confirmed, you can click the green button that says create repository.

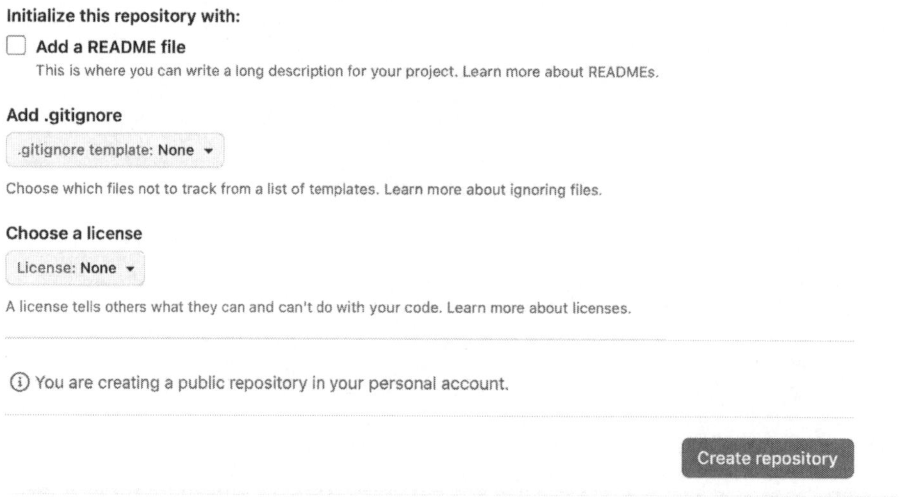

Initialize this repository with:

☐ **Add a README file**
    This is where you can write a long description for your project. Learn more about READMEs.

Add .gitignore

[.gitignore template: None ▾]

Choose which files not to track from a list of templates. Learn more about ignoring files.

Choose a license

[License: None ▾]

A license tells others what they can and can't do with your code. Learn more about licenses.

ⓘ You are creating a public repository in your personal account.

[Create repository]

Figure 1.5: Click Create Repo

Once you have a repo, the next thing you may want to do is to create folders and files. You can click on Add File on the upper right hand corner of the screen as can be seen in the next figure. This Add File is not a button but a drop down. Here you have the option of adding files with upload. Or to create a file.

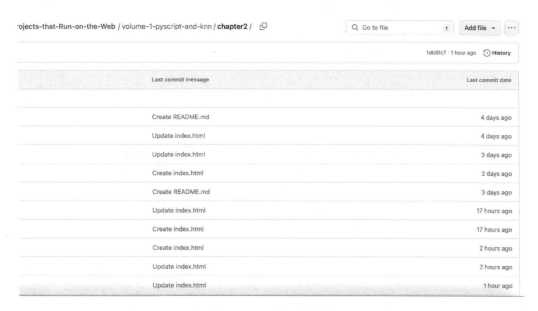

Figure 1.6: Create File

GitHub allows you to create folders and files in the same manner using this Add File drop down. So, if you just do "index.html" it will only create a file. But if you do "my_folder/index.html", then it will create both the folder and the file together. In the next figure you can see that I am creating a folder called "my_folder".

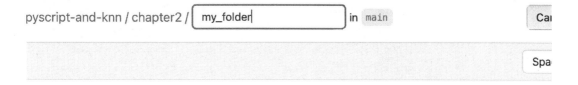

Figure 1.7: Create a folder

The below figure shows the folder is created and followed by the file "index.html". You use the forward slash to indicate the end of the folder name and the beginning of the file name. You can also add your code or text in the blank canvas area below the name.

Figure 1.8: Create index.html file

Finally, click the green button to commit the changes. Commit is the terminology to update your code repo.

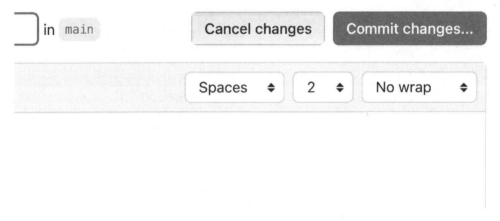

Figure 1.9: Hit Commit

Now, assuming that you have created the file, you can come back to modify it by click the file and then clicking the pencil button on the upper right hand corner as can be seen in the figure below.

Figure 1.10: Click Pencil to edit

This opens the white canvas and you can edit your code. Once done, click the green button to commit your changes.

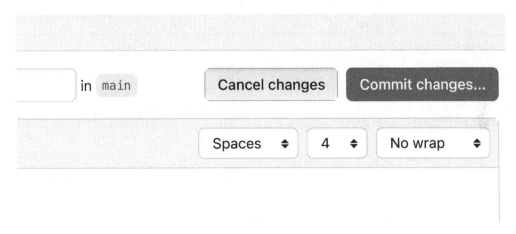

Figure 1.11: After editing index.html you can hit commit

In the next section I will describe GitHub Pages.

1.2.3 Configuring GitHub Pages

In this section we will learn how to configure GitHub Pages. This will allow our HTML files with PyScript to be found on the internet using regular urls. Usually, the url is just your GitHub user name followed by github.io followed by the full path to your repo and your html files. To start configuring Pages, select your repo. In the image below you can see my repo for this book series. Click it.

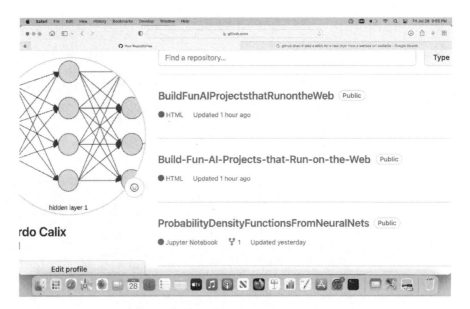

Figure 1.12: The Repo

After selecting the repo, go to the upper right hand corner and click on settings. You need to be signed in to do all of this. This will take you to a new page where you can find the link to Pages.

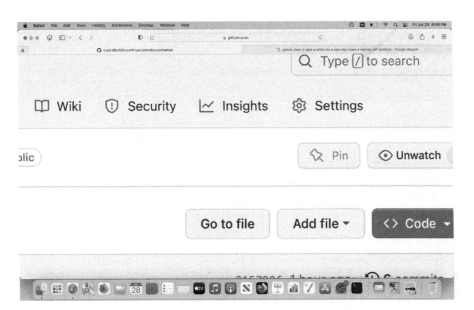

Figure 1.13: Click Settings

Now look for a link called "Pages" as can be seen in the image below. It is usually in the left side of the page. Click it.

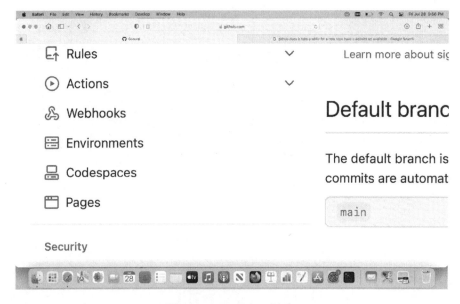

Figure 1.14: Pages Link

Once in the GitHub Pages page, set all drop downs to look like the screen shot below. Basically, deploy from a branch and set to main. Click "save". This process may take a few seconds. In general, Pages is not always instantaneous. Sometimes you load or update an HTML file and it takes 10 minutes for the change to take effect. Also, HTML files will not run until GitHub Pages is configured.

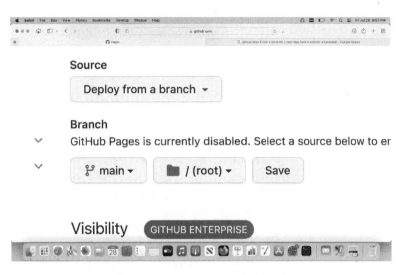

Figure 1.15: Deploy from branch

Your screen should look like this and you should have a url for your account similar to the figure below. What I like to do after getting the url is to create a README.md file and add the url there. That way you can just click on the link and you do not have to remember it.

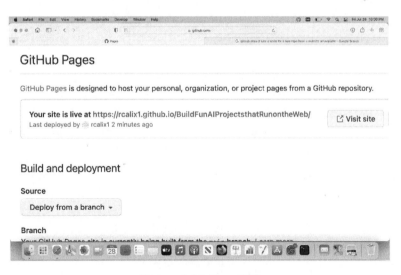

Figure 1.16: Your URL

This should conclude our GitHub discussion.

1.3 HTML

HTML is what makes the internet run. HTML stands for Hyper Text Markup Language and it was invented at the dawn of the internet. It has proven to be very versatile and useful. You use it to create web pages with nice buttons and text boxes. I will not cover all of HTML of course and instead only cover the parts required to complete this simple project. The basic principle in HTML is that of encapsulation. You say this is an HTML document by using a pair of open and close HTML tags. Closing tags are the ones that have the forward slash before the keyword.

HTML code looks like this:

Listing 1.1: HTML code

```
<html>
<body>

.... your code goes here

</body>
</html>
```

Those are in fact the tags that surround everything else. HTML tags can encapsulate many other types of tags but the 2 main tags are the HEAD tags and the BODY tags. HEAD tags are usually for configurations, styles, or functions you can call. BODY tags are for adding elements to your site such as textboxes, images, buttons, and many, many other things.

1.4 JavaScript

Whereas HTML is static, JavaScript is dynamic. What that means is that JavaScript runs on the browser dynamically and can be used to dynamically change a website. We actually will not use a lot of JavaScript in this project since we will be using PyScript instead. To use

JavaScript we usually include a new set of tags in our HTML code. The tags are **<script>** and **</script>** like in the listing below.

Listing 1.2: HTML with JavaScript tags

```
<html>
<head>
     <script>

          ... you can add JavaScript here

     </script>
</head>
<body>

     ....your code goes here

</body>
</html>
```

1.5 PyScript

As I previously described, PyScript (Anaconda, 2021) is like JavaScript but for running Python code on the web browser. It consists of a set of tags that we use to enclose Python code. It supports powerful Python libraries like Numpy and Pandas. Wow! You can do a lot with these. JavaScript is its own very powerful language and you can do a lot with it. Python is an amazing programming language but it was not made to run on web browsers like JavaScript. That is why PyScript has been created. It allows you to write the same Python code but on the browser as long as it is enclosed in PyScript tags. So, PyScript is not a new programming language to learn. If you already know Python, then you will be able to unleash all your knowledge in the browser very quickly. If you do not know Python, do not worry. It is super easy to learn. There are many, many tutorials on line. I even have some videos on learning Python in my YouTube channel. So, you can also try those.

The PyScript configuration tags are used to list libraries like Numpy and Pandas. The following are the PyScript configuration tags:

<py-config> and **</py-config>**

And the following tags are the heart of it all. They are the PyScript tags where you write your actual Python code. They are as follows:

<script type="py"> and **</script>**

The following code listing provides an example of their usage.

Listing 1.3: PyScript Tags

```
<html>
<head>
        <script>
                ... you can add JavaScript here
        </script>
</head>
<body>

        <py-config>
                        ...libraries like numpy and pandas are listed here
        </py-config>

        <script type="py">

                        ...your python code

        </script>
</body>
</html>
```

1.6 Python

Python is a programming language. It is used quite extensively for data science, AI, and machine learning. But Python does not run on a web browser. So, with Python alone, we cannot deploy our AI models on a browser. That is why we need PyScript. PyScript allows us to write Python code but inside HTML code that runs on a browser. In the next figure, I show how to add simple Python code inside PyScript tags. Do not worry about the Python code for now. In chapter 2, we will do many examples using Python and Numpy with PyScript before we actually build our Project in chapter 3. So, you will get some additional practice with just Python and Numpy.

The following code listing shows an example of using Python with PyScript. With this simple Python code, we create a variable, a Python list, and print the word **hello**.

Listing 1.4: Numpy inside PyScript tags

```html
<html>
<head>
      <script>
                ... you can add JavaScript here
      </script>
</head>
<body>
       <py-config>
                    ...libraries like numpy and pandas are listed here
       </py-config>

       <script type="py">

                a = 3
                list_of_numbers = [1, 2, 3, 4, 5]
                print("Hello")

       </script>
</body>
</html>
```

1.7 Numpy

I was very, very impressed when I first learned that you can run Numpy in PyScript. Numpy is the math and linear algebra library for Python. You can do a lot of physics and math with Numpy. It is very efficient and runs fast. This is what sold me on PyScript. Before getting to KNN in chapter 3, I will do a few fun examples with Numpy and PyScript in chapter 2 just to illustrate its almost infinite power. Okay, maybe not infinite, but I love Numpy :)

The code listing below is similar to previous examples. We add Numpy instructions but we need to invoke the Numpy library first. This can be seen in the code listing. The following statement is used to invoke libraries in Python.

import numpy as np

We create the object **np** which is what we reference every time we want to use Numpy. Here, the Python list is now converted to a Numpy array and then printed. Later we will see that instead of the **print** statement, we will want to display Python data with HTML tags such as the **div** tag.

Listing 1.5: Add Numpy library and code with PyScript

```html
<html>
<head>
    <script>
            ... you can add JavaScript here
    </script>
</head>
<body>
    <py-config>
            numpy
    </py-config>
     <script type="py">

                import numpy as np
                a = np.array([4,5,2,6,8])
                print(a)

    </script>
</body>
</html>
```

1.8 Pandas

If Numpy was the cake, then Pandas was the icing on the cake. I really like Pandas as well for data science. It is like having a very powerful Microsoft Excel for manipulating your data. We will mostly use it in this project to read in the data. However, in future volumes, you will no doubt see it again. I have not used too much Pandas in this book, or other libraries for that matter, as I wanted to keep things simple.

1.9 Data

The term machine learning means that the machine, in this case the computer through your browser, running an algorithm, needs to learn from something. So, here we will need some data. AI models can use all kinds of data and future books in the series will show examples of other datasets; but for now, we will start with the classic which is Fisher's Iris Flower dataset (Fisher, 1936).

This dataset includes 150 samples. Each sample is for a flower and it is represented by 4 characteristics of the flower. The 4 features are for the length and the width of the sepals and petals, in centimeters, of each plant (in data science we can call them samples). There are three types (or classes) of plants which are Setosa, Virginica, and Versicolor.

1	sepal_length	sepal_width	petal_length	petal_width	species
2	5.1	3.5	1.4	0.2	setosa
3	4.9	3.0	1.4	0.2	setosa
4	4.7	3.2	1.3	0.2	setosa
5	4.6	3.1	1.5	0.2	setosa
6	5.0	3.6	1.4	0.2	setosa
7	5.4	3.9	1.7	0.4	setosa
8	4.6	3.4	1.4	0.3	setosa

Figure 1.17: Iris Dataset

In machine learning, you spend a lot of time processing the data and this can be a difficult part of the process. But, that is also what you want to learn how to do. That is why we love Pandas and Numpy. They make this process so much more easy.

1.10 What is KNN anyway?

Finally, we get to KNN. KNN is the AI algorithm. In chapter 3, I will describe the algorithm itself with code and we will deploy it to the web. KNN stands for the K nearest neighbors algorithm. In essence, it is used for classification. Imagine a space where you have many balls. Some are soccer balls, others are baseballs, others are basketballs, tennis balls, etc. They are all floating in this space. Each ball is described by a specific set of characteristics called features. Some balls are smaller than others, etc. Some are greener than others. The main idea is that similar balls in this space will be closer to each other. Imagine all the bigger balls on the top left side of the space and all the smaller balls on the lower right side of the space as can be visualized in the figure below.

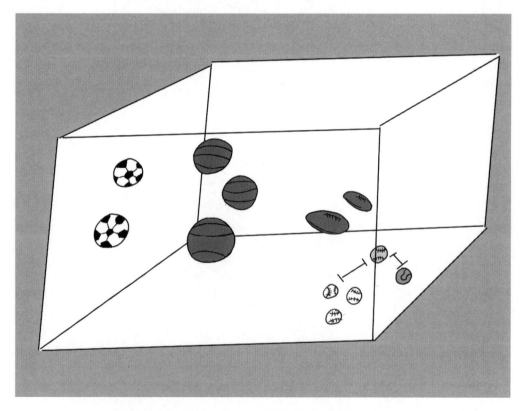

Figure 1.18: Vector Space with balls for different sports

Now, when we add a new ball in this space, its features will force it to be closer to the balls that have similar features to it. This number of features can be 2 or 3 or 10 or 784 or more. Our cubic space of balls in the figure only has 3 features or dimensions. But there is no limit to the number of features or dimensions. The Iris dataset for instance would exist in a space of 4 dimensions. Even though we can't visualize it, the coding and math holds.

Think of each feature as an axis in this space. If we view the space of balls in the figure we immediately know what the ball is. But since AIs do not have eyes (yet), they have to rely on other methods. In this case, KNN should solve this problem. Look at the figure again. In the lower right hand corner of the space there are 3 white baseballs and one green tennis ball. And then there is an odd looking ball with the shape of a baseball and the color of a tennis ball. What is it? That is what KNN tries to solve. Is this odd looking ball closer to green balls or baseball shaped balls? The values of the features are what help KNN to solve this problem.

Okay, that is it for the theory and ideas behind KNN. Now let us introduce the AI project.

So, what will you build? For this first project book in the series, your final application (App) should look like this:

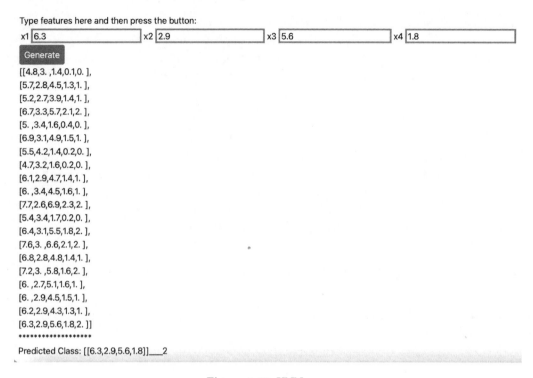

Figure 1.19: KNN app

As you can see, it will be a website with textboxes where you can enter 4 values for the 4 features of a sample of Iris flower. Given those values, KNN will tell you if it is of type Setosa, Virginica, or Versicolor.

1.11 Resources

This project book comes with a companion GitHub repository. All the code files and data can be accessed from there. You can run the websites from there as well via links in the README files. I recommend using the project book as much as possible and only looking at the GitHub files when you are stuck. Solving problems on your own will help you to learn more effectively. Color images are also available from the repo.

The links to the resources are as follows:

- https://github.com/rcalix1/Build-Fun-AI-Projects-that-Run-on-the-Web
- https://www.rcalix.com

I may use my website at https://www.rcalix.com to post additional materials, links, or blog posts, but in general, the GitHub repo should be the official companion site for the book series. As time permits, I may also post related videos on my YouTube channel.

1.12 Conclusion

This concludes chapter 1. In it I described a lot of the background on the tools and the development environment that we will use to build our AI project. We also started to discuss the project goals and some of the key ideas. In chapter 2 we will get into more details about PyScript and how to use it with Python and Numpy. And in chapter 3, we will proceed to build, run and deploy our KNN project to the web.

2 Coding with HTML and PyScript

The focus of this chapter is to build up your skills before starting to implement the KNN algorithm in chapter 3. First, we will develop a simple website that uses PyScript. This will be the equivalent of building your first Hello World application. After that, I will show you some examples of the power of PyScript by doing some exercises which include Python and Numpy code. These exercises will gradually help you to better grasp coding in Python with Numpy, and will help you to better understand how to run everything on the browser with PyScript.

Objective: To write my first Hello World program with PyScript.

The chapter has 2 basic sections. One section focuses on creating your first Hello World program. The second section consists of a set of exercises to get more comfortable with Numpy and PyScript. I often give exercises like these to my machine learning students. I often recommend that they should type up the code themselves (instead of copying) and run it line by line. I feel that by doing this one can develop a type of muscle memory. Hopefully, after doing many of these problems, you will start to become more comfortable with how Numpy works with Python.

So, in summary, this chapter will focus on the following tasks:

■ Build a Hello World program with HTML and PyScript
■ Practice and appreciate the power of Numpy and PyScript

This chapter assumes that you have completed chapter 1, and that you have now completed the setup of your GitHub account and completed all other related configurations.

2.1 Hello World program with HTML and PyScript

The following code listing shows the entire program using HTML, PyScript, and Python. So, what is Hello World anyway? Hello World is usually the first program you write in any programming language. In this listing, I show all the code you need to run Hello World. I do this so that you can see the big picture and so that you get a sense of how big it is. Running this program will write "Hello World" to your website. The results can be seen in the figure after the listing.

Listing 2.1: Hello World code

```html
<html>
    <head>
        <title>Hello World</title>
        <meta charset="utf-8" />

        <link rel="stylesheet" href="https://pyscript.net/latest/pyscript.css"/>
        <script defer src="https://pyscript.net/latest/pyscript.js"></script>
    </head>

    <body>
        <nav class="navbar" style="background-color: #000000">
            <div class="app-header">
                <a class="title" href="" style="color: #f0ab3c">Hello World</a>
            </div>
        </nav>

        <div>Press the button to print hello world </div>
        <button id="get-time" py-click="my_gen_function()" class="py-button">
            Generate </button>

        <p id="current-val"></p>
        <div id="test-output"></div>

        <section class="pyscript">
            <div id="mpl"></div>

                <py-config>
                    packages = []
                    plugins = ["https://pyscript.net/latest/plugins/python/py_tutor.
                        py"]
                </py-config>

                <script type="py">

                    def my_gen_function():
                        ## Element('test-output').element.innerText =   text
                        Element('mpl').element.innerText = "Hello World"

                </script>
        </section>

    </body>
</html>
```

The listings following the next figure in this section will focus on the different parts of the Hello World rogram. It will make it easier for me to discuss what each part is doing. Your Hello World program should look like this when you finish and run it:

Press the button to print hello world

Generate

Hello World

Figure 2.1: Hello World output

In the next listing, I will only discuss the head section of the code denoted by the head tags: **<head> ... </head>**. The title tag **<title>** is used to provide a title for your website and is useful for search engine indexing. The **<meta charset="utf-8" />** is used to define character encoding for your website. The next 2 lines are very important and we will be using them on all our programs. They are both provided by the PyScript project (Anaconda, 2021). The line denoted by the **<link>** tag references the stylesheet which is a file with extension .css. This style sheet just makes our website look more slick when it is running. We could do without it or create our own. But let us just use what the PyScript project provided. CSS files are especially formatted files where we define common things realted to style about our website like fonts, positioning, colors, etc. The last line with the **<script>** tag is required. It imports pyscript.js. Websites can import many other code modules from the internet. This helps to extend their capabilities. So, websites import these .js files. This **pyscript.js** file will help us to run PyScript on our browser.

Listing 2.2: Hello World code - head section

```html
<html>
    <head>
        <title>Hello World</title>
        <meta charset="utf-8" />
        <link rel="stylesheet" href="https://pyscript.net/latest/pyscript.css"/>
        <script defer src="https://pyscript.net/latest/pyscript.js"></script>
    </head>

    ...

</html>
```

The following code listing shows the navbar segment. This is what provides a navigation bar at the top of the page. Here, it is used mostly for presentation. You can ignore this part or consider removing it once you understand how the code works. It is a good exercise to test your understanding. This nav bar can work in conjunction with the .css file we previously discussed.

Listing 2.3: Hello World code the nav tag

```html
<html>

    ...

    <body>
        <nav class="navbar" style="background-color: #000000">
            <div class="app-header">
                <a class="title" href="" style="color: #f0ab3c">Hello World</a>
            </div>
        </nav>

        ...

    </body>
</html>
```

The next listing shows the part of the Hello World code related to triggering events. There are 2 **div** tags, one **p** tag, and one **button** tag. The **p** tag defines paragraphs in your website. You can reference the **p** tag by its **id=current-val**. In general, tags can have ids so they can be referenced. As we will see later, we can call our tags by **id** and write something to them. The **div** with **id=test-output** can be used in the same way. Notice the first **div** does not have an **id** and it is just used to write out some instructions to the website once it is running.

Okay, I saved the best for last. The button tag (**\<button\>**) is used to create a button on your
website. When you press the button, it will call the function name **my_gen_function()**.
Notice that it is associated with the **py-click** option. This means that this is a function written
in Python. And just like that, this is how from HTML, we can call Python code. Now all that
remains is to encapsulate our python code. We will see that in the next code listing.

Listing 2.4: Hello World code - divs and buttons

```
<html>
    ...
    <body>
        ...

        <div>Press the button to print hello world </div>
        <button id="get-time" py-click="my_gen_function()"   class="py-button">
            Generate </button>

        <p id="current-val"></p>
        <div id="test-output"></div>

        ...

    </body>
</html>
```

We have now made it to PyScript! In the next code segment you can see that we have
made it to the section we wanted to get to. This section is encapsulated within the **\<section class="pyscript"\>** tags. This section includes a div (**\<div id="mpl"\>\</div\>**) with **id**
equal to **"mpl"**. Similar to the previous divs, we can select this div by id and write data to it.
In fact, we will write Hello World to this div, but you can write to the other divs as well and
I recommend you try to do just that as an exercise.

The next part in the code is denoted by the **\<py-config\>** tag. You can use this to add any
packages you want into the list packages = []. In the future, we will add packages like Numpy,
etc. Finally, we have made it to the tag where we actually write our Python code. The tag
is called **\<script type="py"\>**. It is a script tag just like for JavaScript but with type "py",
which you guessed it, stands for Python. And inside this tag we can define all the python
code we want. Here, we define the function **my_gen_function()** that is invoked by pressing

29

the button. The rules of Python apply here such as indentation. Make sure all your Python code here has the exact same indentation or you will have errors and will need to debug. The Python syntax is the same.

PyScript provides keywords that you can use in the Python code so that Python can interact with the HTML and the website itself. One such keyword is **Element**. Notice here that **Element** grabs the div with id=mpl and assigns to its "innerText" attribute the text "Hello World". And that is it. This is how PyScript and HTML work together to run Python code on the browser. I recommend that you now go try what you learned and build and deploy your Hello World program from your own repo.

Listing 2.5: Hello World code - PyScript tags

```html
<html>
    ...

    <body>
        ...

        <section class="pyscript">
            <div id="mpl"></div>

            <py-config>
                packages = []
                plugins  = []
            </py-config>

            <script type="py">
                def my_gen_function():
                    ## Element('test-output').element.innerText = text
                    Element('mpl').element.innerText = "Hello World"

            </script>
        </section>

    </body>
</html>
```

That concludes the Hello World program discussion. Even though most of our websites going forward will include these same sections, I will not discuss or describe them again. Instead, going forward I will only focus on the PyScript section and specifically in the Python or Numpy code. I will describe any new PyScript or HTML elements as needed.

2.2 The Power of Numpy and PyScript

In this section, I will present some of the most useful techniques used in this book, or in the deep learning field as a whole, for dealing with data. In general, we want to be very efficient in our processing of the data so we do not use Python lists and "for" loops for everything. Instead, we use Numpy to process tensors in very efficient and clever ways. Numpy borrows many techniques from a field of mathematics called linear algebra. Numpy arrays of different dimensions (scalars, vectors, matrices, hyper-matrices) are more generally referred to as tensors.

The advantage of this approach is that we can perform a lot of linear algebra based math operations like the matrix multiplication, the transpose, etc. on our data using Python's Numpy library. I will not go into any linear algebra theory. Instead, the best way to learn about this approach for AI projects is to do a series of exercises. Eventually you can study the math background if you want to. And because you already have examples of its use, you will be more motivated to study it. I will start with simple examples of Numpy array operations and then move to more complex operations. Along the way, I will point out some terminology or concepts from math.

As previously described, this section assumes you have completed chapter 1. In this chapter, I will mainly focus on describing the Python and Numpy code that goes inside the PyScript section of the HTML code. For a few examples, I will include the whole HTML code, but as we move through the material, I will include less and less of the HTML and just focus on the specific parts we want to cover.

Okay, so let's get started. In the following code listing we import numpy as np. Then we initialize a Numpy array with values [4 5 2 6 8]. The statement

text = str(a)

converts the array to a string and we can finally display it on the website using the statement:

Element('mpl').element.innerText = text

Listing 2.6: Initialize numpy array and display it on website

```html
<html>
    <head>
        <title>First Numpy Example</title>
        <meta charset="utf-8" />
        <link
            rel="stylesheet"
            href="https://pyscript.net/latest/pyscript.css"
        />
        <script defer src="https://pyscript.net/latest/pyscript.js"></script>
    </head>

    <body>
        <div>Press Button</div>
        <button id="get-time" py-click="my_gen_function()" class="py-button">
            Generate</button>

        <section class="pyscript">
            <div id="mpl"></div>

                <py-config>
                    packages = [
                            "pandas",
                            "numpy"
                    ]
                    plugins = []
                </py-config>

                <script type="py">

                    import numpy as np

                    def my_gen_function():
                        a = np.array([4,5,2,6,8])
                        text = str(a)
                        Element('mpl').element.innerText =    text

                </script>
        </section>
    </body>
</html>
```

In the next code listing we do the same as before but we initialize the array to type float.
Notice that we provide a Python list and change the data type with the **dtype** field.

Listing 2.7: Numpy array of floats

```html
<html>
    ...

    <body>
        <div>Press Button</div>
        <button id="get-time" py-click="my_gen_function()"  class="py-button">
            Generate</button>

        <section class="pyscript">
            <div id="mpl"></div>

                <py-config>
                    packages = [
                            "pandas",
                            "numpy"
                    ]
                    plugins = []
                </py-config>

                <script type="py">

                    import numpy as np

                    def my_gen_function():

                        a = np.array([1, 3, 2, 5], dtype='float32')
                        text = str(a)
                        Element('mpl').element.innerText =   text

                </script>
        </section>
    </body>
</html>
```

You can see that the values can now have decimal points. This gives us [1. 3. 2. 5.] and pressing the button calls the function **my_gen_function** which runs the Numpy code. Again, the array is converted to a string and assigned to the div with **id** equal to **mpl** using the following code segment:

Element('mpl').element.innerText = text

The following figure shows the result of running this in the browser.

33

Press Button

Generate

[1. 3. 2. 5.]

Figure 2.2: Numpy array of floats

Going forward, to reduce copying too much repetitive code, I will only discuss and show the parts inside the PyScript section denoted by:

<section class="pyscript"> </section>

Everything else should be the same.

A Numpy matrix (2D np array) can be declared like so:

list_of_lists = [[1, 2, 3], [4, 4, 5] , [6, 2, 11]]

This Python list can be converted to a Numpy array using **np.array()**. The following listing shows the code sequence and how to assign it to the "mpl" div.

Listing 2.8: Numpy Matrix

```
<section class="pyscript">
    <div id="mpl"></div>

        <py-config>
            packages = [
                    "pandas",
                    "numpy"
            ]
            plugins = []
        </py-config>

        <script type="py">

            import numpy as np

            def my_gen_function():

                list_of_lists = [[1, 2, 3], [4, 4, 5] , [6, 2, 11]]
                a = np.array(list_of_lists)
                text = str(a)
                Element('mpl').element.innerText =   text

        </script>
    </section>
```

Running this code gives us a 3x3 matrix as can be seen in the following figure.

Figure 2.3: Numpy Matrix

Numpy has special functions to initialize a matrix. In the next code listing, three Numpy tensors are created. The first generates a Numpy array of size 10 made up of all zeros like so:

[0 0 0 0 0 0 0 0 0 0]

This is achieved with the following code segment:

b1 = np.zeros(10, dtype=int)

The second tensor consists of a 4x6 matrix of all ones. This is achieved with the Numpy statement:

b2 = np.ones((4, 6), dtype=float)

The final tensor is a 3x3 matrix where all the values are 42. This is achieved with the statement:

b3 = np.full((3, 3), 42)

Listing 2.9: Initialize 3 matrices

```
<html>
    ...
    <body>
        <div>Press Button</div>
        <button id="get-time" py-click="my_gen_function()"  class="py-button">
            Generate </button>
        <section class="pyscript">
            <div id="mpl1"></div>
            <div id="mpl2"></div>
            <div id="mpl3"></div>
                <py-config>
                    packages = ["pandas", "numpy"]
                    plugins = []
                </py-config>
                <script type="py">
                    import numpy as np
                    def my_gen_function():

                        b1 = np.zeros(10, dtype=int)
                        text1 = str(b1)
                        Element('mpl1').element.innerText =  text1

                        b2 = np.ones((4, 6), dtype=float)
                        text2 = str(b2)
                        Element('mpl2').element.innerText =  text2

                        b3 = np.full((3, 3), 42)
                        text3 = str(b3)
                        Element('mpl3').element.innerText =  text3
                </script>
        </section>
    </body>
</html>
```

Notice that the code now includes 3 div tags with ids: **mpl1**, **mpl2**, and **mpl3**. The 3 tensors are assigned to each of these div tags, respectively. The results can be seen in the following figure.

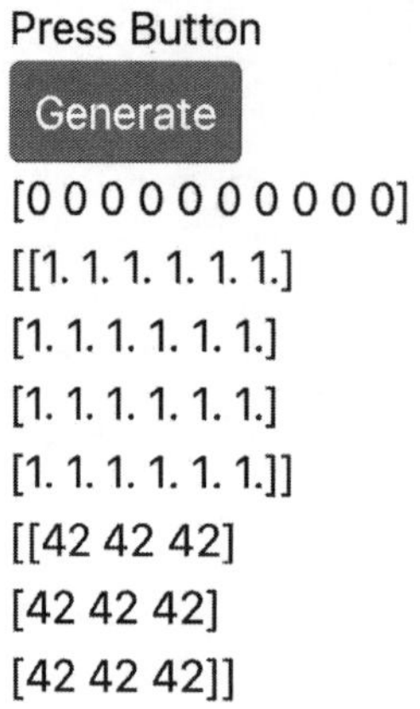

Press Button

Generate

[0 0 0 0 0 0 0 0 0 0]
[[1. 1. 1. 1. 1. 1.]
[1. 1. 1. 1. 1. 1.]
[1. 1. 1. 1. 1. 1.]
[1. 1. 1. 1. 1. 1.]]
[[42 42 42]
[42 42 42]
[42 42 42]]

Figure 2.4: Numpy Initialization

Sometimes we need Numpy arrays with different data in them. Numpy has quick ways of creating arrays with different data in them. The **np.arange** function is useful for this. For example, in the following listing, the code creates a Numpy array with 10 values in the range from 1 to 28 with a step of size 3 like so:

[1 4 7 10 13 16 19 22 25 28]

The function **np.linspace** is another way of generating Numpy arrays with data in them. Here, we generate 20 data points from 0 to 1 spaced by a step size of around 0.05.

Listing 2.10: Initialize Sequences

```
<html>
    ...

    <body>
        ...
        <section class="pyscript">
            <div id="mpl1"></div>
            <div id="mpl2"></div>
                <py-config>
                    packages = ["pandas", "numpy"]
                    plugins = []
                </py-config>
                <script type="py">

                    import numpy as np
                    def my_gen_function():

                        b1 = np.arange(1, 30, 3)
                        text1 = str(b1)
                        Element('mpl1').element.innerText =  text1

                        b2 = np.linspace(0, 1, 20)
                        text2 = str(b2)
                        Element('mpl2').element.innerText =  text2

                </script>
        </section>
    </body>
</html>
```

The results of using **np.arange()** and **np.linspace()** can be seen in the following figure. Go ahead and calculate the differences between each number and the next and you will find that they equal the step size.

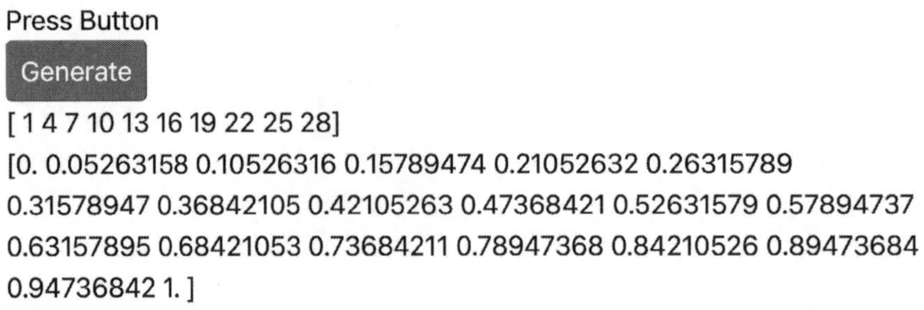

Press Button

Generate

[1 4 7 10 13 16 19 22 25 28]
[0. 0.05263158 0.10526316 0.15789474 0.21052632 0.26315789
0.31578947 0.36842105 0.42105263 0.47368421 0.52631579 0.57894737
0.63157895 0.68421053 0.73684211 0.78947368 0.84210526 0.89473684
0.94736842 1.]

Figure 2.5: Numpy Initialization sequences

The following code listing introduces us to some of Numpy's random functions. With

np.random.random((4, 4))

we can generate random data in the form of a 4x4 matrix with random values.

If we want random data with a mean of 0 and standard deviation of 1 we can write:

np.random.normal(0, 1, (4,4))

Here, we get a 4x4 matrix of random data with mean 0 and standard deviation 1.

Finally, to get the dimensions of matrices we can use **.shape**, **.ndim**, **.size**. In our below code listing, this is done with the following statements:

text3a = str(b3a.ndim)

text3b = str(b3b.shape)

text3c = str(b3c.size)

Listing 2.11: Numpy random initialization and shapes

```
<html>
    ...
    <body>
        ...
        <section class="pyscript">
            <div id="mpl1"></div>
            <div id="mpl2"></div>
            <div id="mpl3"></div>
                <py-config>
                    packages = ["pandas", "numpy"]
                    plugins = []
                </py-config>
                <script type="py">
                    import numpy as np
                    def my_gen_function():
                        b1 = np.random.random((4, 4))
                        text1 = str(b1)
                        Element('mpl1').element.innerText = text1

                        ## mean 0 and standard deviation 1
                        b2 = np.random.normal(0, 1, (4,4))
                        text2 = str(b2)
                        Element('mpl2').element.innerText = "******" + "\n" + text2

                        b3a = np.random.randint(20, size=6)
                        b3b = np.random.randint(20, size=(3,4))
                        b3c = np.random.randint(20, size=(2,4,6))
                        text3a = str(b3a.ndim)
                        text3b = str(b3b.shape)
                        text3c = str(b3c.size)
                        Element('mpl3').element.innerText = text3a + "\n" + text3b +
                            "\n" + text3c
                </script>
        </section>
    </body>
</html>
```

The result of running the previous Numpy code on the browser can be seen in the figure below. The dimensions from **.shape**, **.ndim**, and **.size** can be seen at the bottom of the figure.

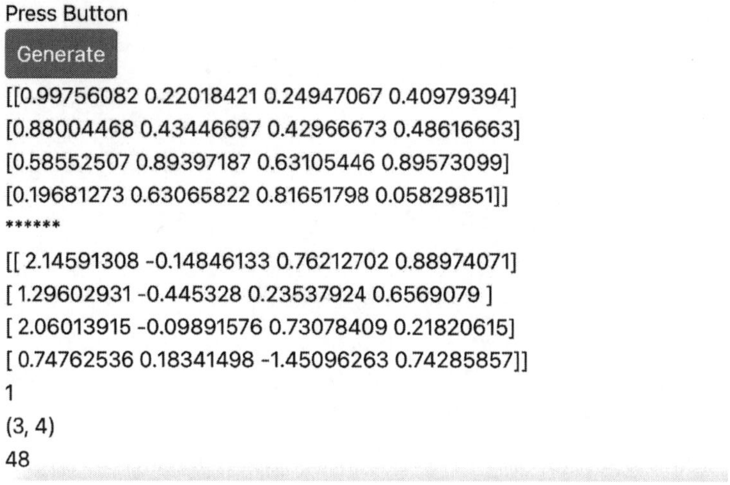

Press Button

Generate

[[0.99756082 0.22018421 0.24947067 0.40979394]
[0.88004468 0.43446697 0.42966673 0.48616663]
[0.58552507 0.89397187 0.63105446 0.89573099]
[0.19681273 0.63065822 0.81651798 0.05829851]]
******
[[2.14591308 -0.14846133 0.76212702 0.88974071]
[1.29602931 -0.445328 0.23537924 0.6569079]
[2.06013915 -0.09891576 0.73078409 0.21820615]
[0.74762536 0.18341498 -1.45096263 0.74285857]]
1
(3, 4)
48

Figure 2.6: Numpy random initialization and shapes

Knowing how to index a Numpy array is very important. The following code listing shows different ways of indexing a Numpy array. Indexing just means extracting values from the Numpy array or matrix by index value. For example, for the vector

[1. 3. 2. 5.]

We can get the following by index:

First value 1.0

Third value 2.0

Last value 5.0

Before last value 2.0

The next code listing shows the use of indexing for each of the previously mentioned cases.

Listing 2.12: Indexing

```html
<html>
    ...
    <body>
        ...
        <section class="pyscript">
            <div id="mpl1"></div>
            <div id="mpl2"></div>
            <div id="mpl3"></div>
                <py-config>
                    ...
                </py-config>
                <script type="py">
                    import numpy as np
                    def my_gen_function():

                        b1 = np.array([1, 3, 2, 5] , dtype='float32' )
                        text1 =  str(b1) + "\n"
                        text1a = "first "          + str( b1[0]  ) + "\n"
                        text1b = "third "          + str( b1[2]  ) + "\n"
                        text1c = "last "           + str( b1[-1] ) + "\n"
                        text1d = "before last " + str( b1[-2] ) + "\n"
                        Element('mpl1').element.innerText =  text1 + text1a + text1b
                            + text1c + text1d

                        b2 = np.array([[1, 2, 3, 4],
                                       [5, 6, 7, 8],
                                       [9, 10, 11, 12]] )
                        text2 = str(b2) + "\n"
                        text2a = "first " + str( b2[0,0] )    + "\n"
                        text2b = "last " + str( b2[2, -1] )    + "\n"
                        Element('mpl2').element.innerText =  "******" + "\n" + text2
                            + text2a + text2b
                </script>
        </section>
    </body>
</html>
```

We can also index matrices. The statements

b2[0,0] and **b2[2, -1]**

are examples of indexing matrix b2 as defined in the previous code listing. The results can be
seen in the following figure.

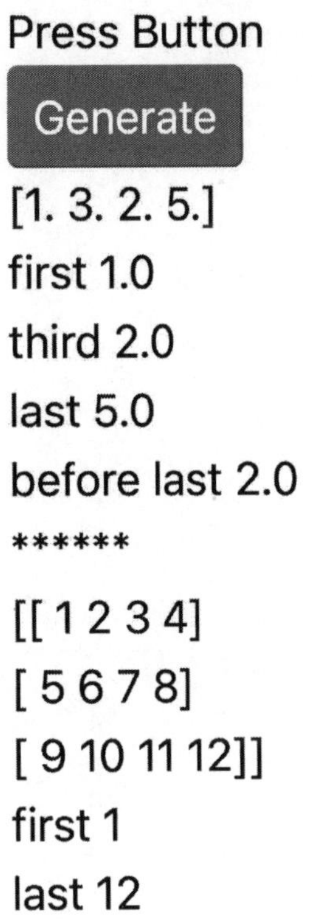

Press Button

Generate

[1. 3. 2. 5.]

first 1.0

third 2.0

last 5.0

before last 2.0

******

[[1 2 3 4]

[5 6 7 8]

[9 10 11 12]]

first 1

last 12

Figure 2.7: Numpy Indexing

One important concept when dealing with Numpy arrays or tensors is slicing. I was almost tempted to create a section just for slicing since it is so important. However, given that it is just another Numpy operation, I decided not to do that. That being said, slicing is very important and you will use it a lot. So, instead of giving it a whole section, I decided to make it a cake. Here it is.

Figure 2.8: Slicing a cake

Slicing helps us to extract slices of data from a vector, matrix, or any other tensor, like extracting 2 middle column vectors in a matrix. We can slice any tensor. As previously mentioned, Tensor is the generic name for an array of any dimension. From a vector to hyper dimensional matrices.

Let us do an example with a vector. Given a Numpy array **x** with 15 values like so:

[0 1 2 3 4 5 6 7 8 9 10 11 12 13 14]

How can you get the following?

a) The first 4 elemets: [0 1 2 3]

b) All values after 3: [3 4 5 6 7 8 9 10 11 12 13 14]

c) All even indeces: [0 2 4 6 8 10 12 14]

d) All uneven indeces: [1 3 5 7 9 11 13]

e) The reverse: [14 13 12 11 10 9 8 7 6 5 4 3 2 1 0]

Once you understand slicing, you will be able to do all that and it will be really easy. The following code listing shows the programming statements to do just that. And the figure after shows the results.

Note: Whenever we want the last value of a matrix, vector, or tensor, we can just use the -1 index.

Listing 2.13: Numpy Slicing

```
...
<script type="py">
    import numpy as np
    def my_gen_function():

        b1 = np.arange(15)
        text1  =   str(b1) + "\n"
        text1a  = "first 4 elemets "    + str( b1[:4]    ) + "\n"
        text1b  = "all after 3 "        + str( b1[3:]    ) + "\n"
        text1c  = "even indeces "        + str( b1[::2]    ) + "\n"
        text1d  = "uneven indeces "    + str( b1[1::2] ) + "\n"
        Element('mpl1').element.innerText =   text1 + text1a + text1b + text1c +
            text1d

        b2 = np.array([[1,  2,  3,  4],
                       [5,  6,  7,  8],
                       [9, 10, 11, 12]] )
        text2   = "***" + "\n" + str(b2) + "\n"
        text2a = "***" + "\n" + "b2[:2,:2] "   + "\n"   + str(b2[:2,:2] ) + "\n"
        text2b = "***" + "\n" + "b2[-1,:-2] "   + "\n"   + str(b2[-1,:-2]) + "\n
            "
        Element('mpl2').element.innerText =   "***" + "\n" + text2 + text2a +
            text2b
</script>
...
```

As we can see in the previous code listing, the answers are as follows:

a) For the first 4 elements we can use: **b1[:4]** where the colon indicates range from blank (the start) to 4.

b) For all after 3 we can use: **b1[3:]** where 3 is the start and the colon indicates range until blank (the end).

c) For all even indeces we can use **b1[::2]** where the first colon indicates the range from start to finish. The second colon indicates a step of 2.

d) For all uneven indeces we can use **b1[1::2]** where this is the same as before but the start is at 1 instead of zero. Remember that in Python, array indeces start at 0.

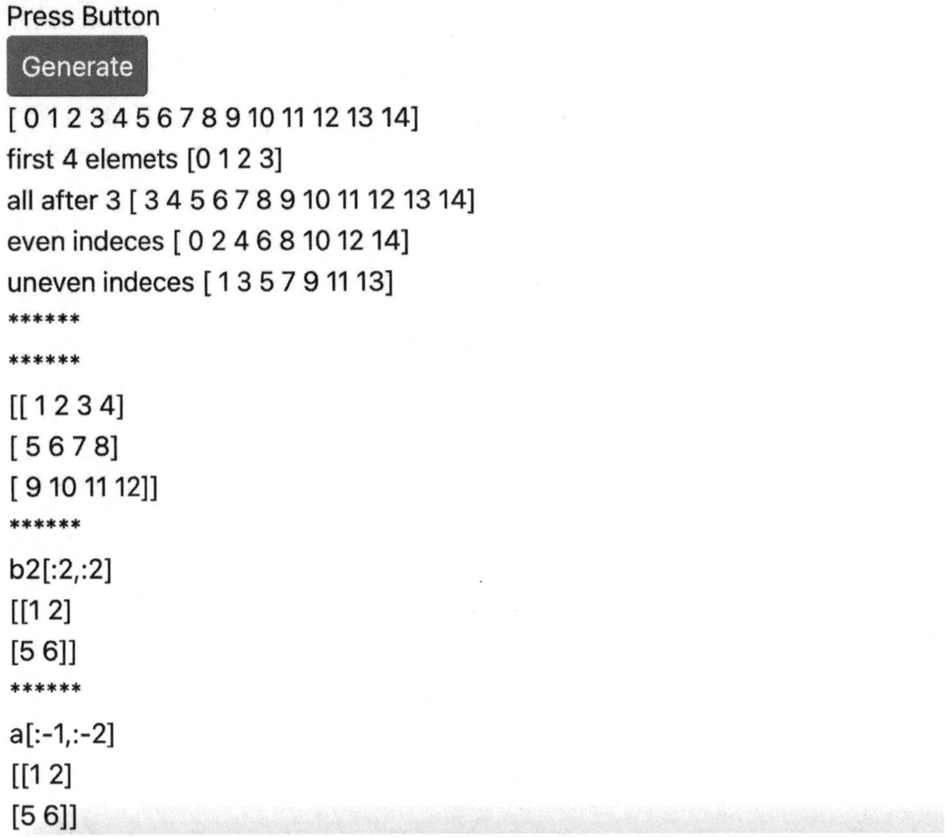

Press Button

Generate

[0 1 2 3 4 5 6 7 8 9 10 11 12 13 14]

first 4 elemets [0 1 2 3]

all after 3 [3 4 5 6 7 8 9 10 11 12 13 14]

even indeces [0 2 4 6 8 10 12 14]

uneven indeces [1 3 5 7 9 11 13]

******

******

[[1 2 3 4]

[5 6 7 8]

[9 10 11 12]]

******

b2[:2,:2]

[[1 2]

[5 6]]

******

a[:-1,:-2]

[[1 2]

[5 6]]

Figure 2.9: Numpy Slicing

For the matrix **b2** in our previous code listing, we can slice it with **b2[:-1,:-2]** and get a 2x2 matrix as can be seen in the Numpy Slicing figure.

2.3 Solve these Problems

Okay, so I have given you a lot of examples. As this is a project and work book, how about you try to implement a few Numpy and PyScript problems on your own. For the following I will provide the problem description and the working Python and Numpy code. What you have to do is to run it on your Browser using PyScript and make sure it works correctly as required by the problem.

2.3.1 Problem 1

In the following code listing we want to slice the second column (column 1). The statement

a[:, 1]

should do it, and the answer should be:

[2 6 10]

Go ahead and deploy this to your GitHub repo.

Listing 2.14: Slicing - All rows of the second column

```
a = np.array ([[1 , 2, 3, 4],
               [5, 6, 7, 8],
               [9, 10, 11, 12]] )

print(a)
print("column1")
print(a[:, 1])
```

2.3.2 Problem 2

In the following code listing we want to slice the second row (row 1). The statement

a[1, :]

should do it, and the answer should be:

[5, 6, 7, 8]

Go ahead and deploy this to your GitHub repo.

Listing 2.15: Slicing - extract a row vector

```
a = np.array([ [1, 2, 3, 4],
               [5, 6, 7, 8],
               [9, 10, 11, 12] ] )

print(a)
print("row1")
print(a[1, :])
```

2.3.3 Problem 3

Okay, that is it for slicing. Now let us try a few other things. The next problem is about reshaping. In the following code listing, we first initialize a vector "a" with 9 values like so

[1 2 3 4 5 6 7 8 9]

We then reshape it into "b" with **a.reshape((3,3))**. This gives us the matrix:

Listing 2.16: Reshaped 3x3 matrix

```
[[1 2 3]
 [4 5 6]
 [7 8 9]]
```

Go ahead and deploy this to your GitHub repo.

Listing 2.17: Numpy Reshaping

```
a = np.arange(1, 10)
b = a.reshape( (3,3) )
print(a)
print(b)
```

2.3.4 Problem 4

Besides using the reshaping operation, we can sometimes use **np.newaxis**. The **np.newaxis** function is critical when we wish to make a row vector into a column vector. The **np.newaxis()** function is used extensibly in Numpy for broadcasting operations (Advanced topic not needed for this project). An example of creating a new axis can be seen in the code listing below. Try it out. Go ahead and deploy this to your GitHub repo.

Listing 2.18: Numpy newaxis

```
v =np.array( [1,2,3,4,5] )
v1=np.array( [5,5,5,5,5] )

m = np.array([[1,  2,  3,  4],
              [5,  6,  7,  8],
              [9,  10, 11, 12]] )

print("reshape as row vector with reshape", v.reshape( (1,5) ))
print("reshape as row vector with newaxis ", v1[np.newaxis, :] )

print("reshape as column vector with newaxis")
print( v1[:, np.newaxis] )

print("reshape matrix_m[:, np.newaxis, np.newaxis, :] with newaxis")
print( m[:, np.newaxis, np.newaxis, :] )
```

2.3.5 Problem 5

Another important Numpy array or tensor technique is concatenation. Natural Language Processing (NLP) approaches use concatenation extensively on some of the models. For example, for language translation and language generation. In the following code listing we see how we can use concatenation with the Numpy function **np.concatenate()**. Try it out. Go ahead and deploy this to your GitHub repo.

Listing 2.19: Numpy concatenation

```
a = np.array([1,2,3,4])
b = np.array([5,6,7,8])
c = np.array([9,10,11])

ab  = np.concatenate( [a, b] )
abc = np.concatenate( [a, b, c] )

print(ab)
print(abc)
```

2.3.6 Problem 6

An example of concatenation with matrices can be seen in the code listing below. Notice the use of **axis=0** to indicate on what dimension to concatenate. Try it out. Go ahead and deploy this to your GitHub repo.

Listing 2.20: Numpy matrix concatenate on dimension 0

```
m1 = np.array([ [1,2,3],
                [4,5,6],
                [7,8,9] ])

m2 = np.array([ [10,11,12],
                [13,14,14],
                [16,17,18] ])

m1_m2_concat = np.concatenate([m1, m2], axis=0)

print(m1_m2_concat)
```

2.3.7 Problem 7

You can concatenate on **axis=1** like in the code listing below. Try it out. Go ahead and deploy this to your GitHub repo.

Listing 2.21: Numpy matrix concatenate on dimension 1

```
m1 = np.array([ [1,2,3],
                [4,5,6],
                [7,8,9] ])

m2 = np.array([ [10,11,12],
                [13,14,14],
                [16,17,18] ])

m1_m2_concat = np.concatenate([m1, m2], axis=1)

print(m1_m2_concat)
```

2.3.8 Problem 8

Obviously, having data means that you want to perform many kinds of math operations on this data. The following are some examples of some of the most common operations. Try it out. Go ahead and deploy this to your GitHub repo.

Listing 2.22: Numpy math operations

```
x = np.array([1,2,3,4])

print(x+10)
print(x-10)
print(x*10)
print(x/2)
print(-x)
print(x ** 3)
print(np.power(4, x))
print(np.log(x))
print(np.log2(x))
print(np.log10(x) )
```

The results of the previous math operations on vector [1 2 3 4] are as follows:

For the operation x+10 we get [11 12 13 14]

For the operation x-10 we get [-9 -8 -7 -6]

For the operation x*10 we get [10 20 30 40]

For the operation x/2 we get [0.5 1.0 1.5 2.0]

For the operation -x we get [-1 -2 -3 -4]

And so on ...

2.4 Conclusion

In this chapter, we learned about the basics of PyScript and HTML. We deployed our first Hello World program on the web. We also covered many problems using Numpy and Python and learned how to deploy them to the web. Now we are ready for chapter 3 which will cover our AI project and how to deploy it to the web.

3 Build your AI Project with KNN and PyScript

This chapter focuses on the development of a simple website that uses PyScript, HTML, Python, Numpy and KNN. This is the main AI portion of the book and the project we are trying to complete and deploy to the web using GitHub. We previously described KNN as the K Nearest Neighbors algorithm. It is our first machine learning algorithm in this book series. KNN is a great algorithm to start your journey into the world of AI. It is simple enough, very useful, and can be coded from scratch efficiently using only a few lines of code with Python and Numpy.

Objective: To write my first AI algorithm (KNN) with PyScript and Numpy.

So, what can KNN do? KNN is what is known as a machine learning algorithm for classification. If you recall, in chapter 1, I gave a quick explanation of KNN using a vector space of different balls used in sports. I said that, in essence, KNN is used for classification. We can imagine a space where you have many balls from different sports. Some are soccer balls, others are baseballs, others are basketballs, tennis balls, etc. They are all floating in this space. Each ball is described by a specific set of characteristics called features. These features can be for color, diameter, shape, number of lines or curves, etc. Some balls are smaller than others, etc. Some are greener than others. The main idea is that similar balls in this vector space will be closer to each other based on these features. Imagine all the bigger balls on the top left side of the space and all the smaller balls on the lower right side of the space as can be visualized in the figure below.

Now, when we add a new ball in this space, its features will force it to be closer to the balls that have similar features to it. This number of features can be 2 or 3 or 10 or 784 or more. Our cubic space of balls in the figure only has 3 features or dimensions. But there is no limit to the number of features or dimensions. The Iris dataset, for instance, would exist in a space of 4 dimensions. Even though we can't visualize it, the coding and math holds.

Think of each feature as an axis in this space. If we view the space of balls in the figure, we immediately know what the ball is. But since AIs do not have eyes (yet), they have to rely on other methods. In this case, KNN should solve this problem. Look at the figure again. In the lower right hand corner there are 3 white baseball balls and one green tennis ball. And then there is an odd looking ball with the shape of a baseball and the color of a tennis ball. What is it? That is what KNN tries to solve. Is this odd looking ball closer to the green tennis ball or the baseball shaped balls? The values of the features are what help KNN to solve this problem.

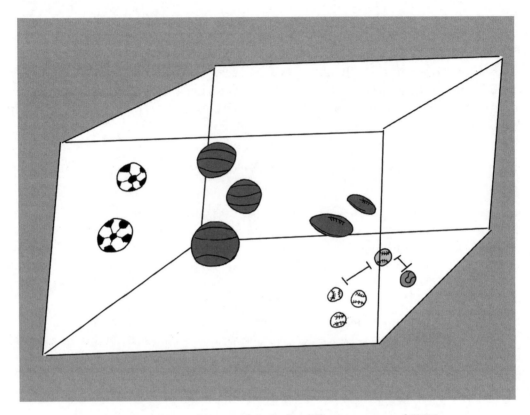

Figure 3.1: Vector Space with balls for different sports and KNN

Basically, KNN will take a sample in question, say the green baseball, and measure the distance between it and all other balls in this space (i.e. the soccer balls, basket balls, football balls, tennis balls, and baseballs). Once KNN calculates all the distances, it will rank then from lowest to highest distance. Out of these ranked distances, it will select the top **k** distances and assign to the ball in question the majority class from the set containing just the top **k** shortest distances. For the given example, if we selected a k=5 then the 5 closest balls to the ball in question (green baseball) would be 3 baseballs, 1 tennis ball, and one football. Since the majority is baseball, KNN would assign the class baseball to our ball in question.

From the figure, that would seem like the right answer. In the next sections, I will proceed to describe how to implement, test, and deploy our KNN machine learning model to the web.

In the next 2 sections, I will describe the KNN algorithm. The first of the 2 sections is the basic implementation of KNN. It involves building the model and running it. Usually this is where you figure out the performance metric of your model. We will still run it on the browser and deploy it but it will not be a general use App where we can add our inputs and do inference. Inference is a term used in AI which usually means prediction. The second of these 2 sections will do just that and use what we learned in the first section to build our inference application. A lot will be the same but it will take data from text boxes and we will need to make changes to execute this new functionality.

In summary, the next 2 sections cover:

■ Basics to get KNN running
■ A KNN app that you can use with user supplied data for Iris flower classification

3.1 Basics to get KNN running

As you may remember from the previous chapters, first we need to define the HTML code that encapsulates the PyScript code, which in turn, encapsulates our KNN algorithm implemented in Python and Numpy. The code in the next code listing should be familiar to you by now. Everything in the head section is similar to what we have previously described. The body section also includes the same **div** tags and the **button** we discussed in chapters 1 and 2.

Listing 3.1: Standard HTML code

```html
<html>
    <head>
        <title >HTML code for KNN</title >
        <meta charset="utf-8" />
        <link
            rel="stylesheet"
            href="https:// pyscript.net/latest/pyscript.css"
        />
        <script defer src="https:// pyscript.net/latest/pyscript.js"></script>
    </head>

    <body>
        <div>Press Button</div>
        <button id="get-time" py-click="my_gen_function ()"  class="py-button">
            Generate </button>

        <div id="test -output"></div>

        <section class="pyscript">

                    ...the bulk of the Python code

        </section>
    </body>
</html>
```

In the next code listing we can see the previously discussed PyScript section denoted by

<section class="pyscript">

This section contains the previously discussed 3 items: the **div** with **"mpl"** id we have used before, the **config** section for libraries we want to use, and the **<script type="py">** section where we write out actual Python and Numpy code.

Listing 3.2: PyScript section with HTML tags

```
<section class="pyscript">

            <div id="mpl"></div>

            <py-config>
                packages = [
                        "pandas",
                        "matplotlib",
                        "numpy"
                ]
                plugins = []
            </py-config>

            <script type="py">

                ..the python code

            </script>
</section>
```

In the next code listing, you can see all the code needed to run KNN. Wow! Pretty short right? This code splits our data into **train** and **test** sets. Then grabs every sample in the test set and compares it to every sample in the train set. As previously described, for each test sample, we get all distances between the test samples and all train samples. We then rank them and select the top **K** distances. Finally, we assign the majority class associated for the top 5 distances. That is it!

Listing 3.3: The whole KNN code

```
<section class="pyscript">
    <div id="mpl"></div>
        ...

        <script type="py">

            import numpy as np
            import pandas as pd
            import matplotlib.pyplot as plt
            import matplotlib.tri as tri
            From pyodide.http import open_url

            def euclidean_distance(v1, v2):
                return np.sqrt( np.sum(    (v1 - v2)**2    )   )

            def predict(test_x):
                k = 5
                distances = [ euclidean_distance(test_x , x)  for x in X_train     ]
                k_neighbor_indices = np.argsort(distances)[:k]
                labels = [ y_train[i]  for i in k_neighbor_indices   ]
                labels_np = np.array( labels   )
                pred = int( np.mean(labels_np)   )
                return pred

            url1 = ("https://rcalix1.github.io/Build-Fun-AI-Projects-that-Run-on-the-
                Web/volume-1-pyscript-and-knn/chapter3/knn/iris.csv")
            iris_pd = pd.read_csv(open_url(url1))
            iris_pd['species'] = iris_pd['species'].replace({'setosa':0, 'versicolor'
                :1 , 'virginica':2})
            iris_np = iris_pd.to_numpy()

            np.random.shuffle(iris_np)

            X_train    = iris_np[1:130, :4]
            y_train    = iris_np[1:130,  4]
            X_test     = iris_np[130:150, :4]
            y_test     = iris_np[130:150, 4]

            def my_gen_function():
                accum_res = ""
                for i, test_x in enumerate( X_test ):
                    the_pred = predict(test_x)
                    text1 = np.array2string( test_x , precision=2, separator=',',
                        suppress_small=True)
                    text2 = str( y_test[i] )
                    text3 = str( the_pred )
                    accum_res = accum_res + text1 + "_" + text2 + "_" + text3 + "\n"
                Element('mpl').element.innerText =   accum_res

        </script>
</section>
```

Okay, so I always like to see the big picture first. And that is what the previous code listing was for. Now we can proceed to break the code down into the various parts and describe what they are doing.

In the next code listing we can see all the libraries needed for our KNN implementation. We have Numpy, Pandas, Pyodide, and Matplotlib. Numpy as you know by now is for all the math. Pandas is used in this project book to read in the data. Pyodide is intrinsic to PyScript and it is very important to run Python on the web. Matplotlib is not used in this project book but it is very important for AI research. You will be amazed in future project books by its capabilities for data visualization.

Listing 3.4: Libraries needed for KNN

```
<section class="pyscript">
            <div id="mpl"></div>

        . . .

            <script type="py">

                import numpy as np
                import pandas as pd
                import matplotlib.pyplot as plt
                import matplotlib.tri as tri
                from pyodide.http import open_url

            </script>
</section>
```

The next section in the code includes a function called the Euclidean distance as can be seen in the next code listing.

Listing 3.5: Insert code directly in your document

```
<section class="pyscript">
        <div id="mpl"></div>

            <script type="py">

        ...

            def euclidean_distance(v1, v2):
                return np.sqrt( np.sum(    (v1 - v2)**2    )    )

        ...

            </script>
        </section>
```

This is the function that measures the distance between 2 points in a vector space. These 2 point need to have the same size but the size can be of any dimension. For instance, for our Iris data, every point has 4 features. So in the code the 2 points v1 and v2 would be of size 4 each. However, we could also have points (samples) of many more dimensions. For instance, points with 100 features. So in this case v1 and v2 would both need to have size 100. But the cool thing is that the function for distance calculation would still work. That is the power of Numpy.

The name Euclidean distance comes from a Greek philosopher named Euclid. He is best known for putting together one of the earliest books on geometry. The book was so good for its time that the type of mathematics it discussed became known as Euclidean geometry.

So, where does this magical Euclidean distance function come from? Would you believe that it is related to an idea one of the great Greek philosophers (Pytagoras) is credited with? Pytagoras was before Euclid and is credited with coming up with the Pythagorean Theorem (bubble in the figure).

Figure 3.2: Pythagoras

The theorem states that given a triangle (see figure below), the sum of the areas of the two squares on the legs (a and b in green) equals the area of the square on the hypotenuse (c in green).

If you look closely at the figure below, you can see that I have written down the connection between Pythagoras' theorem, and the euclidean function we used in our code.

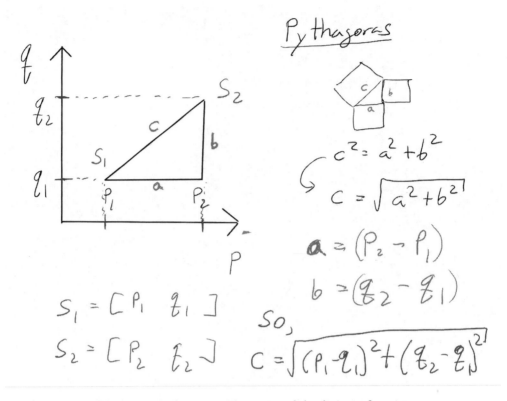

Figure 3.3: Pythagorean Theorem and the distance function

Now, with some of the math history out of the way, let us continue with our code description. In the next code listing we can see the KNN **predict** function. Actually, the **predict** function is the actual KNN algorithm. I will describe it in detail next. The variable **test_x** is the sample in question. Say, one Iris test sample with 4 features (**[x1, x2, x3, x4]**). The next line of code:

distances = [euclidean_distance(test_x , x) for x in X_train]

calculates all the distances between **test_x** and all the training samples. The way this statement is written is called a list comprehension in Python. The **"for x"** part of the statement means that each sample in the train set is grabbed and passed to the **euclidean_distance** function along with the test sample. Both points are passed to the Euclidean equation and the distance between them is returned. This is done for every training sample and in the end, the list **"distances"** contains all the measured distances.

The next statement:

k_neighbor_indices = np.argsort(distances)[:k]

takes all the distances and, using **np.argsort()**, sorts them. Then we slice the sorted vector with **[:k]**. This slicing only returns the indeces for the k smallest distances. The indeces are assigned to the variable named **k_neighbor_indices**. One important note is that argsort returns only the indeces in the vector and not the values themselves. Since the indeces in the "X" data and "y" labels are aligned, then we can use these same indeces to extract the corresponding labels from "y". And that is exactly what we do with the following statement:

labels = [y_train[i] for i in k_neighbor_indices]

Finally, the list **labels** is converted into a Numpy array of the labels which are numbers, and the mean of them is calculated. That is it. You have found the label.

Listing 3.6: The KNN predict function

```
<section class="pyscript">
        <div id="mpl"></div>

            <script type="py">

            ...

                def predict(test_x):
                    k = 5
                    distances = [ euclidean_distance(test_x , x)  for x in
                        X_train   ]
                    k_neighbor_indices = np.argsort(distances)[:k]
                    labels = [ y_train[i]  for i in k_neighbor_indices  ]
                    labels_np = np.array( labels  )
                    pred = int( np.mean(labels_np)  )
                    return pred

            ...

        </script>
    </section>
```

Wasn't that easy. We have described the whole KNN algorithm. Wow!

Now let us proceed to talk about the data. As previously described, we are using the Iris dataset. The file is provided in the companion GitHub repo for this project book. It is stored as a file in .csv format. This is a very common format for AI/ML research and development.

As can be seen in the next code listing, we read the data with Pandas. We then convert the labels from words to numbers, and then convert the Pandas object to a Numpy matrix.

Listing 3.7: Reading in the data

```
<section class="pyscript">
        <div id="mpl"></div>
        ...
        <script type="py">
        ...
            url1 = ("https://rcalix1.github.io/Build-Fun-AI-Projects-that-Run
                -on-the-Web/volume-1-pyscript-and-knn/chapter3/knn/iris.csv")

            iris_pd = pd.read_csv(open_url(url1))

            iris_pd['species'] = iris_pd['species'].replace({'setosa':0, '
                versicolor':1 , 'virginica':2})

            iris_np = iris_pd.to_numpy()
        ...
        </script>
    </section>
```

In the next code listing we shuffle the data using the following statement:

np.random.shuffle(iris_np)

This statement randomizes the rows in the iris Numpy array. Randomizing the data is a standard step in AI/ML research and development.

Listing 3.8: Shuffle the data

```
<section class="pyscript">
        <div id="mpl"></div>
          ...
          <script type="py">
            ...

            np.random.shuffle(iris_np)

            ...
          </script>
</section>
```

The code in the following code listing is not necessary but it can be handy to view and debug the data. I recommend that you try it out and view the details about the data. The trick is to take Numpy data and display it on the web page. To do that we can use statements such as this one:

Element('test-output').element.innerText = text

Here you can see that **"Element"** grabs HTML tags by id ('test-output'), and can assign to its **"innerText"** field, a string from Python passed in the variable **"text"**.

Listing 3.9: Debug and view data

```
<section class="pyscript">
          <div id="mpl"></div>

          ...

          <script type="py">

          ...

              ## This is just used to view and debug the data or code

              ## look at shape
              ## text1 = str(iris_np.shape)

              ## look at data
              ## str_iris_np = np.array2string(iris_np, precision=2, separator
                  =',', suppress_small=True)
              ## text2 = str(str_iris_np)

              ## text = text2
              ## Element('test-output').element.innerText =   text

          ...

          </script>
     </section>
```

Since you are a **slicing** master by now, the following code listing should be starting to make sense. The following code listing shows how to slice the Iris Numpy array into 4 new Numpy arrays. In machine learning you usually have **train** and **test** sets, and for convenience for each set (train and test), we want to have, for each row, the feature data in "**X**", and the labels data in "**y**". That is why we get 4 new Numpy tensors. It is more convenient and practical. Basically, all of chapter 2 was developed just so that you can understand this part of the code :)

Listing 3.10: Slicing the data into Train and Test

```
<section class="pyscript">
        <div id="mpl"></div>
          ...
           <script type="py">
         ...

               X_train    = iris_np[1:130, :4]
               y_train    = iris_np[1:130,  4]

               X_test     = iris_np[130:150, :4]
               y_test     = iris_np[130:150, 4]


        ...

          </script>
</section>
```

The following code listing is similar to our previously described debugging code segment. The code is not necessary and that is why it is commented out with the pound side. But you can use it if you wish to display the data to the website (debugging).

Listing 3.11: To look at the data

```
<section class="pyscript">
     <div id="mpl"></div>
       ...
        <script type="py">
          ...
          ## str_np = np.array2string( X_train, precision=2, separator=',',
               suppress_small=True)
          ## str_np = np.array2string( y_train, precision=2, separator=',',
               suppress_small=True)
          ## str_np = np.array2string( X_test, precision=2, separator=',',
               suppress_small=True)
          ## str_np = np.array2string( y_test, precision=2, separator=',',
               suppress_small=True)
          ## text = str(str_np)
          ## Element('test-output').element.innerText =  text
          ...
        </script>
</section>
```

We finally get to our last function which is:

my_gen_function()

This is the function that is invoked when you press the button of your website. Some would call it an event handler. As can be seen in the following code listing, the function has a **"for"** loop which grabs, for every iteration, a vector in **X_test**. Each value from **X_test** will be compared to every valued in **X_train** (i.e. calculate the Euclidean distance). In the next section when we build our inference KNN app, we will not use this **"for"** loop since we will pass the test sample from values collected with text boxes.

Now back to the code. For every iteration of the **"for"** loop, we pass **test_x** to the predict function. As previously described, this function returns the label into the variable

"the_pred"

And that is it. After that we just convert the **"x"** data and predicted label to a string. Using the **"Element"** object, we grab the div tag with **id="mpl"** and display our data there on the website. That is it!

Listing 3.12: My Generate Function

```
<section class="pyscript">
    <div id="mpl"></div>
        ...
        <script type="py">
            ...
        def my_gen_function():
            accum_res = ""
            for i, test_x in enumerate( X_test ):
                the_pred = predict(test_x)

                text1 = np.array2string( test_x , precision=2, separator=',',
                    suppress_small=True)
                text2 = str( y_test[i] )
                text3 = str( the_pred )
                accum_res = accum_res + text1 + "___" + text2 + "___" + text3 + "\n"
            Element('mpl').element.innerText =  accum_res
        </script>
</section>
```

We are done describing KNN. In the next section, I will just describe the additional statements we need to make to complete and deploy our KNN website.

3.2 A KNN app for Iris Flower classification

In this section you will bring everything together and build the web site that runs KNN. Since
this is a KNN based AI model for classifying Iris flowers, all our input samples will have 4
features. The input features can be entered into 4 text boxes. When you press the button,
the application will convert the 4 values into a list. The list will be converted into a Numpy
array (i.e. a vector). And then, finally, through the KNN algorithm, the model will predict
the class. In this section I will only describe the parts of the code that are different from what
was described in the previous section.

While I like to look at all the code as a whole, the whole AI App for Iris classification is too
big to fit here. The companion book repo on GitHub includes the file with all the code in
it. However, I would recommend that you try to build the KNN Iris classification website
yourself from the parts. There really isn't too much code that is new or different from what
was described in the previous section.

Listing 3.13: The text boxes

```
<html>
<body>
<div>Type features here and then press the button: </div>

<table>
<tr>
    <td>x1 </td>
    <td> <input type="text" style="border:3px solid #F7730E;" value="3" id="
        testInput1"/> </td>

    <td> x2 </td>
    <td>    <input type="text" style="border:3px solid #F7730E;" value="3" id="
        testInput2"/> </td>

    <td> x3 </td>
    <td>    <input type="text" style="border:3px solid #F7730E;" value="2" id="
        testInput3"/> </td>

    <td> x4 </td>
    <td>    <input type="text" style="border:3px solid #F7730E;" value="3.4" id="
        testInput4"/> </td>
</tr>
</table>

<button id="get-time" py-click="my_gen_function()"  class="py-button">Generate </
    button>

<div id="test-output"></div>

<section class="pyscript">
    ....

</section>

</body>
</html>
```

One of the main things we need to add is 4 text boxes. That is really easy to do. HTML has a special tag called <input> that we can use for this purpose. We make sure to give an id name to each of the 4 input text boxes so we can reference them in the code to get the values. To better display the text boxes, we enclose them in a table which can also be constructed on a website using HTML. This is shown in the previous code listing.

The next new piece of code can be seen in the following code listing. We need to obtain the values from the text boxes and convert then into one single Numpy array of size 4 (for the

four features). Here once again we use the **"Element"** object to grab the values in the 4 text
boxes by **id** name. We then create a Python list with the values like so:

conditions_list = [c1, c2, c3, c4]

we then convert the list into a Numpy array. As previously described, the statement is:

np_conditions_list = np.expand_dims(np_conditions_list, axis=0)

which can convert our Numpy array from shape (4,) to shape (1, 4). This will help us when
we calculate the Euclidean distance ensuring the vector has the proper arrangement of dimensions that Numpy expects.

Listing 3.14: Get the data from text boxes and convert to numpy vector

```
<script type="py">
    ...

        def get_np_conditions_vector():
            c1 = float( Element('testInput1').element.value )
            c2 = float( Element('testInput2').element.value )
            c3 = float( Element('testInput3').element.value )
            c4 = float( Element('testInput4').element.value )

            conditions_list = [c1, c2, c3, c4]
            np_conditions_list = np.array(conditions_list)
            np_conditions_list = np.expand_dims(np_conditions_list, axis
                =0)

            return np_conditions_list

    ...

</script>
```

The final code listing is for our new **my_gen_function()**. Now we modify it to read the data
from the text boxes. Notice the call to:

test_x = get_np_conditions_vector()

This gets the data from the text boxes and assigns it as a Numpy vector to **test_x**. After that, the code is pretty much the same as before.

Listing 3.15: Gen Function that reads from text boxes

```
<script type="py">

    ...

    def my_gen_function():
        test_x = get_np_conditions_vector()
        the_pred = predict(test_x)
        text1 = np.array2string( test_x , precision=2, separator=',',
            suppress_small=True)
        text3 = str( the_pred )
        accum_res = "***\n" + "Predicted  Class: " + text1 + "__" + text3 + "\n"
        Element('mpl').element.innerText =  accum_res

    ...
</script>
```

Well, that is it! The next figure shows what the final website should look like. For your convenience I have displayed in the website all the test samples with their associated classes. If you notice, each row is a vector of 5 values separated by comma. The first four values are the 4 features ([**x1, x2, x3, x4**]), and the fifth value is the label. You can use this to make sure your model is predicting correctly. Since it should not have seen the test samples before, it is possible that the model could make a few mistakes. However, if it is a good model, for the majority of the cases, the predicted class should match the real class. With this idea, could you devise a metric to quantify performance? You can call it the accuracy metric.

Note: you will get a few mis-classifications. But out of 30, it should be less that 5.

As an example, I grabbed the last test sample. I entered the 4 features into the text boxes, and the KNN model predicted the class 2. If you look at the last data row in the figure, you can see that the label is also 2. Therefore, the model was accurate for that test sample.

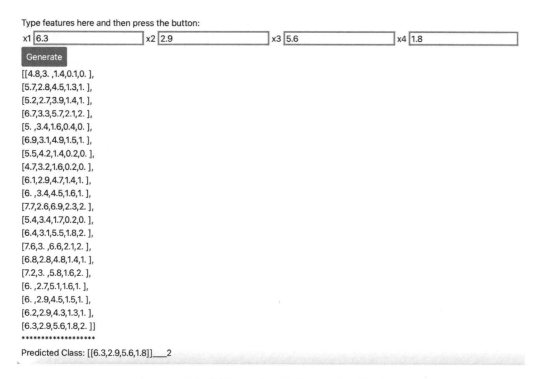

Figure 3.4: KNN app for Iris flower classification

3.3 Conclusion

This concludes this chapter. You have completed all the tasks and built and deployed your KNN website which can do Iris Flower classification. If you have not already realized it, you can build KNN models for other datasets or for your own data and problems. I hope this Volume 1 in the series sparks your imagination. I can't wait to hear what new applications you develop from the concepts in this book.

4 Final Conclusions

This is the conclusion of the book. I hope you enjoyed it. I think this is only the beginning of what can be done with AI and the web. Sure, many startups and big companies alike are working really hard to make AI a part of our daily lives. My goal with this book is for this knowledge to be shared with everyone instead of with just a few.

In the future, I plan to make more volumes in this series. In general, they will always be focused on one specific project you as the reader can build. With this project book I have only begun to scratch the surface.

One future topic I am currently working on is Neural Networks which build on many interesting ideas of machine learning. So, stay tuned.

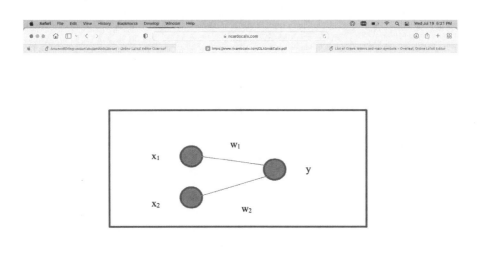

Figure 4.1: Nets

4.1 Where to go from here?

You can definitely wait for future volumes in this series. However, if you just cannot wait, you can study PyScript on your own. There are many resources being created everyday. AI and machine learning move at a super fast speed and things are changing constantly so do not be surprised if PyScript changes a little bit or a lot. This is a constant in this field. You have to learn to adapt and be quick.

Until the next one!

Other Books by Ricardo A. Calix

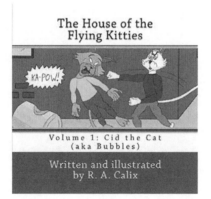

You can check out my previous books at https://www.rcalix.com/mybooks.htm or contact at **rcalix@rcalix.com**.

The Author: Ricardo A. Calix

 Dream Big.

Ricardo A. Calix was born in La Ceiba, Honduras, on June 11th, 1978. He received the B.S. degree in industrial and systems engineering from Universidad Tecnologica Centroamericana, Tegucigalpa, Honduras, in 2001. He received a masters degree from Louisiana State University (LSU), Baton Rouge, in 2006. He was a graduate assistant in the department of industrial engineering at LSU from 2007 to 2011, where he conducted research in natural language processing. He obtained his Ph.D. degree in Engineering Science with a research focus on natural language processing and machine learning from Louisiana State University, Baton Rouge, in 2011. His research interests include natural language processing, deep learning, industrial modelling and automation, and reinforcement learning. He is currently an associate professor of computer information technology at Purdue University Northwest, and an independent data science consultant.

https://www.rcalix.com

Glossary

G

GITHUB · The *GitHub* web site is an online platform owned by microsoft that allows you to load your code files and static websites. Languages like JavaScript and the PyScript framework are supported on GitHub.

H

HTML · *HTML* stands for the Hyper Text Markup Language. It is the basic coding language you use to build website with nice textboxes and buttons.

K

KNN · *KNN* stands for the K nearest neighbors algorithm. It is one of the traditional machine learning algorithms.

N

NUMPY · *Numpy* is a very powerful python library use for math and linear algebra.

P

PYTHON · Python is an interpreted language used extensively in data science and machine learning.

PYSCRIPT · *PyScript* The *PyScript* framework allows you to run python code in HTML.

Bibliography

Anaconda (2021). *PyScript.* https://github.com/pyscript.

Fisher, R.A. (1936). *The Use of Multiple Measurements in Taxonomic Problems.* Annals of Eugenics, 7, 179-188.

An Important Final Note

Writers are not performance artists. While there are book signings and public readings, most writers (and readers) follow their passion alone in their homes.

*What applause is for the musician, **reviews** are for the writer.*

Books create a community among readers; you can share your thoughts among all those who will or have read the book.

Leave a thoughtful, honest review and help me to create such a community on the platform on which you have acquired this book. *What did you like, what can be improved? To whom would you recommend it?* What else would you like to see in the series?

Thank you, also in the name of all the other readers who will be able to better decide whether this book is right for them or not. A positive review will increase the reach of the book; a negative review will improve the quality of the next book. We welcome both!

" A journey of a thousand miles begins with a single step.

— Chinese Proverb

Printed in Great Britain
by Amazon

29892197R00057